SALAMANDERS
LIVED WITH THE DINOSAURS!

BY HEATHER MOORE NIVER

Gareth Stevens
PUBLISHING

Please visit our website, www.garethstevens.com. For a free color catalog of all our high-quality books, call toll free 1-800-542-2595 or fax 1-877-542-2596.

Cataloging-in-Publication Data

Names: Niver, Heather Moore.
Title: Salamanders lived with the dinosaurs! / Heather Moore Niver.
Description: New York : Gareth Stevens Publishing, 2017. | Series: Living with the dinosaurs | Includes index.
Identifiers: ISBN 9781482456615 (pbk.) | ISBN 9781482456639 (library bound) | ISBN 9781482456622 (6 pack)
Subjects: LCSH: Salamanders–Juvenile literature.
Classification: LCC QL668.C2 N58 2017 | DDC 597.8'5–dc23

First Edition

Published in 2017 by
Gareth Stevens Publishing
111 East 14th Street, Suite 349
New York, NY 10003

Copyright © 2017 Gareth Stevens Publishing

Designer: Laura Bowen
Editor: Therese Shea

Photo credits: Cover, p. 1 (salamander) Martin Shields/Moment/Getty Images; cover, p. 1 (footprints) nemlaza/Shutterstock.com; cover, pp. 1–24 (background) Natalia Davidovich/Shutterstock.com; cover, pp. 1–24 (stone boxes) Daria Yakovleva/Shutterstock.com; p. 5 (top) Shutterstock Premium/Shutterstock.com; p. 5 (bottom) Nashepard/Shutterstock.com; p. 6 Flickr upload bot/Wikimedia Commons; p. 7 (Japanese) Hansmuller/Wikimedia Commons; p. 7 (Chinese) Daniel Heuclin/Nature Picture Library; pp. 8, 10, 21 (Karaurus) ArthurWeasley/Wikimedia Commons; pp. 9 (eggs), 12 Fredlyfish4/Wikimedia Commons; p. 9 (larva with gills) Jacopo Werther/Wikimedia Commons; p. 9 (larva with lungs) Eric Isselee/Shutterstock.com; p. 9 (adult) NatureArtForest/Shutterstock.com; p. 11 Miroslav Hlavko/Shutterstock.com; p. 13 Paul Starsota/Corbis Documentary/Getty Images; p. 15 (main) Tremor Photography/Shutterstock.com; p. 15 (inset) Obsidian Soul/Wikimedia Commons; p. 16 Matt Jeppson/Shutterstock.com; p. 17 John Macgregor/Photolibrary/Getty Images; p. 19 Dotname2469/Wikimedia Commons; p. 21 (fossil) Ghedoghedo/Wikimedia Commons.

Printed in China

CPSIA compliance information: Batch #CW17GS: For further information contact Gareth Stevens, New York, New York at 1-800-542-2595.

CONTENTS

Words in the glossary appear in **bold** type the first time they are used in the text.

SPOT THE SALAMANDER

Salamanders are small creatures you might see on a hike in the woods. You or a friend might even have a pet salamander. If you do, your pet is **related** to some amazing ancient **amphibians**!

Salamanders are sometimes mistaken for lizards. However, lizards are reptiles, while salamanders are amphibians. But these amphibians once lived alongside some famous reptiles: dinosaurs! Keep reading to find out how the salamanders of the dinosaur age were similar to and different from those we know today.

THE PREHISTORIC WORLD

Dinosaurs weren't amphibians. They were reptiles. Modern reptiles usually lay eggs and have skin covered with scales or bony plates. (However, some dinosaurs had feathers!)

4

THE WORD "SALAMANDER" COMES FROM AN ANCIENT GREEK WORD MEANING "FIRE LIZARD." PEOPLE ONCE MISTAKENLY THOUGHT SALAMANDERS COULD SURVIVE FIRE.

marbled salamander

red salamander

TODAY'S SALAMANDERS

First, it's helpful to know about modern salamanders. Salamanders have thin bodies and long tails. They're amphibians, so most spend part of their life in water and part on land. Like reptiles, they're also cold-blooded. That means their body **temperature** changes with the temperature of the **environment**.

Salamanders can be small. The Tennessee pygmy salamander sometimes only grows to be 1.5 inches (3.8 cm) long. Others are larger, such as the Chinese giant salamander, which can be longer than 5.5 feet (1.7 m).

Tennessee pygmy salamander

THE LARGEST LIVING SALAMANDER TODAY IS THE CHINESE GIANT SALAMANDER, SHOWN BELOW. JAPANESE GIANT SALAMANDERS ARE ONLY SLIGHTLY SMALLER.

Japanese giant salamander

Chinese giant salamander

ON LAND AND UNDERWATER

Scientists think salamanders have **adaptations** that helped them survive. Most salamanders are born in water with **gills**, but grow **lungs** to live on land as adults. The hellbender salamander is a bit different. It uses gills to breathe in water for its first 2 years. As adults, hellbenders breathe through their skin!

Other species, or kinds, of salamanders breathe through their skin, too. Adapting new ways to breathe might have been one reason salamanders survived.

Amphibamus

THE PREHISTORIC WORLD

The amphibian *Amphibamus* (am-fih-BAY-muhs) existed about 300 million years ago. It lived in wet areas and probably breathed through its skin like some salamanders today.

SALAMANDER LIFE CYCLE

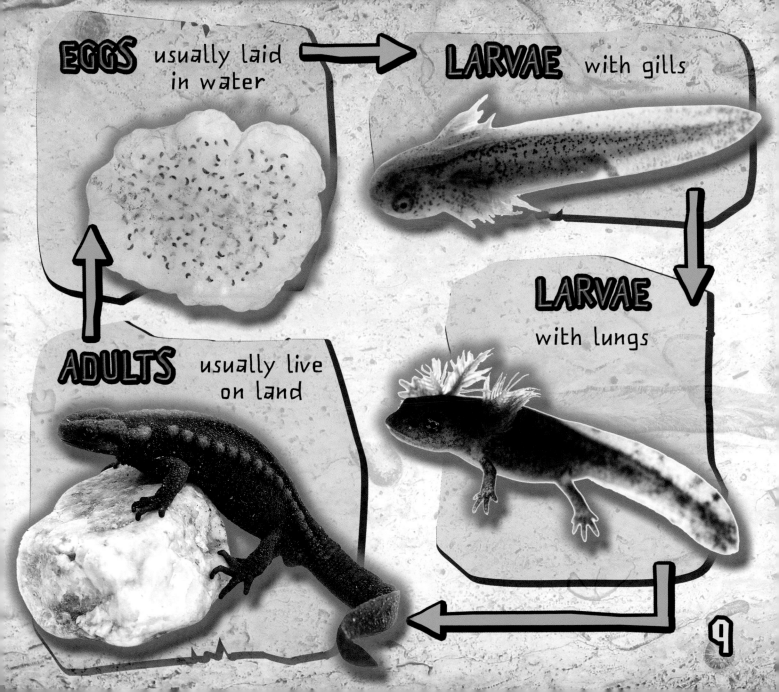

EGGS usually laid in water

LARVAE with gills

LARVAE with lungs

ADULTS usually live on land

9

SALAMANDERS SURVIVE

In hot environments, salamanders may find shade or go underground. They don't want their skin to dry out—or they'd die!

Salamanders can survive cold environments, too. Those in water sometimes stay active under a layer of ice. Others hide in dens. Still others are frozen through the winter! They stop breathing, and their heart stops beating. However, in the spring, the ice melts, and they "come back to life"! This adaptation would have helped salamanders when Earth was very cold.

Microbrachis

THE PREHISTORIC WORLD

Microbrachis was an animal much like a salamander that lived about 300 million years ago. It spent most of its time in water and breathed through gills.

AN ICE AGE IS A PERIOD DURING WHICH TEMPERATURES FALL WORLDWIDE AND LARGE AREAS ARE COVERED WITH ICE. SOME ANIMALS DIED OUT WITH THE START OF THE LAST ICE AGE 2.6 MILLION YEARS AGO, WHILE OTHERS, SUCH AS THE SALAMANDER, SURVIVED.

SCARY SKIN!

Another adaptation for salamander survival is scary skin. If a predator tries to take a bite of a salamander, a body part on the back of the salamander's neck gives off a poison or bad-tasting liquid. The predator often drops the salamander after a taste!

Some salamanders have poison in their tail, which they swing at their attacker. This is called a tail lashing.

The Jordan's salamander gives off a slime that turns into a kind of glue. The glue can trap the attacker for a time!

Jordan's salamander

WHEN THE MUDPUPPY SALAMANDER IS IN DANGER, IT CAN MAKE ITS SKIN EXTRA SLIPPERY AND WIGGLE OUT OF A PREDATOR'S HOLD. IT THEN SWIMS TO SAFETY. UNLIKE MANY SALAMANDERS, MUDPUPPIES LIVE IN WATER ALL THEIR LIFE.

13

TAKE THE TAIL

Salamanders have another special skill. They can grow new body parts. If a predator grabs the tail of a salamander, the tail can separate—and continue to move! The moving tail **confuses** the predator and lets the salamander run to safety. Luckily, the salamander can grow a new tail after a few weeks. It needs its tail for balance.

Salamanders can lose and regrow other body parts, too, such as legs and toes. Being able to regrow body parts helps salamanders survive in environments with many predators.

THE PREHISTORIC WORLD

Tiktaalik (tihk-TAH-lihk) was a cross between a salamander and a fish. It had "fins" with simple fingers. It couldn't walk, but could probably make its way onto land.

A FIRE SALAMANDER'S BRIGHT COLORING TELLS PREDATORS IT'S POISONOUS. HOWEVER, IF THAT DOESN'T WORK, IT CAN LEAVE ITS TAIL BEHIND TO ESCAPE AN ENEMY.

Tiktaalik

LADIES ONLY

Most female salamanders need a male to **fertilize** their eggs in order to produce young. However, some female *Ambystoma* salamanders don't need males to have baby salamanders. These salamanders have adapted to living in environments where there are few male **mates**. They steal matter with **DNA** that males from other salamander species leave behind. Then, they use it to clone, or make copies of, themselves!

Scientists usually think cloned animals are weaker. However, they've found out that *Ambystoma* salamanders regrow their lost tails 1.5 times faster than other salamanders!

barred tiger salamander

SCIENTISTS THINK FEMALE *AMBYSTOMA* SALAMANDERS HAVE BEEN ABLE TO HAVE YOUNG WITHOUT MALES FOR MORE THAN 6 MILLION YEARS! BARRED TIGER SALAMANDERS AND BLUE-SPOTTED SALAMANDERS ARE IN THE *AMBYSTOMA* GROUP.

blue-spotted
salamander

THE SUPERSALAMANDER

In 2015, scientists made a cool discovery—**fossils** of a giant amphibian. About 220 million years ago, an animal similar to a salamander wandered Earth. It was called *Metoposaurus algarvensis*. Scientists sometimes call it the "supersalamander."

While today's salamanders are mostly small, supersalamanders were more than 6.5 feet (2 m) long! They had a mouth full of hundreds of sharp teeth and strong jaws that would snap shut. Scientists think they ate dinosaurs as well as other prehistoric animals.

THE PREHISTORIC WORLD

During the time *Metoposaurus* was on Earth, dinosaurs were much smaller and less fierce than those that would come later, such as *Tyrannosaurus rex*.

THE "SUPERSALAMANDER" MAY HAVE WEIGHED AS MUCH AS AN ADULT HUMAN!

AMPHIBIANS FROM ANCIENT TIMES

Scientists think giant salamander-like amphibians were wiped out during an **extinction** event about 200 million years ago, long before the death of the dinosaurs. Smaller salamanders have survived, but aren't safe from becoming extinct in the future.

Chinese giant salamanders are in danger of dying out because so many people eat them. Other species are in trouble because their homes have been polluted or built over. Scientists think Earth's warming is also causing some salamanders to become smaller. Can salamanders count on humans to help them survive another million years?

NEXT TIME YOU SPOT A SALAMANDER, REMEMBER THAT THEY'RE RELATED TO SOME SCARIER CREATURES THAT HAVE LONG SINCE DIED OUT.

THE PREHISTORIC WORLD

Fossils of the first true salamander, like the ones we know today, were found in Asia. *Karaurus* (kah-ROHR-uhs) was about 8 inches (20 cm) long and probably weighed a few ounces. It lived more than 145 million years ago.

Karaurus

GLOSSARY

adaptation: a change in an animal that better suits conditions

amphibian: an animal that spends part of its life in water and part on land

confuse: to make something uncertain or hard to understand

DNA: matter in the cells of plants and animals that carries information about the makeup of a living thing

environment: the conditions that surround something

extinction: the state that results when something has died out completely

fertilize: to make an egg able to grow

fossil: the hardened marks or remains of plants and animals that formed over thousands or millions of years

gill: a body part used to get oxygen from water

lung: one of the two body parts that people and animals use to breathe air

mate: one of two animals that come together to produce babies

related: belonging to the same group or family because of shared features

temperature: how hot or cold something is

FOR MORE INFORMATION

BOOKS

Bell, Samantha S. *12 Amphibians Back from the Brink.* North Mankato, MN: 12-Story Library, 2015.

Hesper, Sam. *Fire Salamanders.* New York: PowerKids Press, 2015.

Kolpin, Molly. *Salamanders.* Mankato, MN: Capstone Press, 2010.

WEBSITES

Amphibians: Salamander & Newt
animals.sandiegozoo.org/animals/salamander-newt
Discover more about these curious creatures.

Prehistoric Amphibians
www.dkfindout.com/us/dinosaurs-and-prehistoric-life/prehistoric-amphibians/
Learn about all kinds of prehistoric amphibians and other salamander relatives.

Spotted Salamander
www.nwf.org/Wildlife/Wildlife-Library/Amphibians-Reptiles-and-Fish/Spotted-Salamander.aspx
Read fun facts about the spotted salamander.

Publisher's note to educators and parents: Our editors have carefully reviewed these websites to ensure that they are suitable for students. Many websites change frequently, however, and we cannot guarantee that a site's future contents will continue to meet our high standards of quality and educational value. Be advised that students should be closely supervised whenever they access the Internet.

INDEX